GW00597272

Violin
Grade 1

Pieces

for Trinity College London exams

2016-2019

Published by
Trinity College London
www.trinitycollege.com

Registered in England
Company no. 02683033
Charity no. 1014792

Printed in England by Caligraving Ltd.

Bohemia

Polka

Margery Dawe
(died 2001)

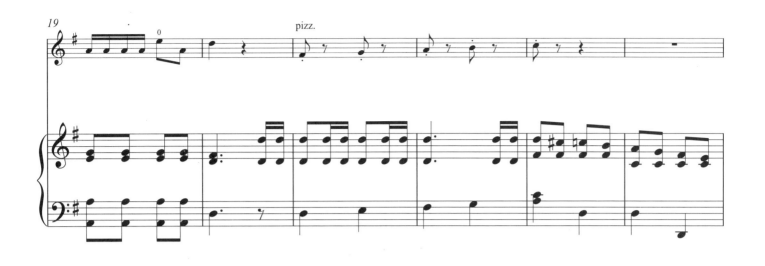

Toodle-pip

Edward Huws Jones
(born 1948)

Dizzy Lizzy Lightweight

Caroline Lumsden (born 1951) &
Ben Attwood (born 1977)

The words should be omitted in the exam.

Menuett

K.105/1

Arr. Ursula Erhart-Schwertmann

Wolfgang Amadeus Mozart
(1756–1791)

Do not play the repeats in the exam.

From: Ursula Erhart-Schwertmann: *Mozart für Violine und Klavier*.

Cha Cha Bowing

Peter Wilson

The Old Castle

Kathy Blackwell (born 1958) &
David Blackwell (born 1961)

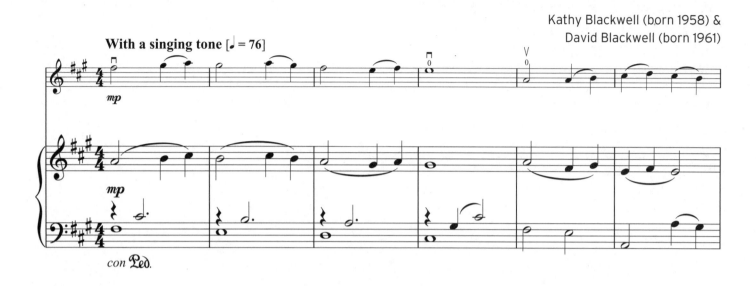

The Old Castle by Kathy and David Blackwell from 'Fiddle Time Joggers'.
© Oxford University Press 1998. Reproduced by permission. All rights reserved.

Minuet

Adam Carse
(1878–1958)

Morning Song

Marjorie Helyer
(1912–1984)

Willow Water

Sheila Nelson
(born 1936)

Do not play the first repeat in the exam.

Ballad for a Rainy Day

Peter Wilson